Map of Andover, 1890

ANDOVER
A Pictorial History

The Right Honourable Jane Elizabeth, Viscountess of Andover, who died on 29 April 1863. One of her ancestors, the Honourable Thomas Howard, KG, second son of the Earl of Suffolk, was created Viscount Andover in 1626. He died in 1660. Today the family seat is at Andover House, Charlton Park, Malmesbury, Wiltshire.

ANDOVER
A Pictorial History

Derek J. Tempero

Phillimore

1991

Published by
PHILLIMORE & CO. LTD.
Shopwyke Hall, Chichester, Sussex

ISBN 0 85033 811 5

Printed and bound in Great Britain by
BIDDLES LTD.,
Guildford, Surrey

List of Illustrations

Illustration Acknowledgements

My thanks are due to the following people who allowed me to borrow their photographs and postcards, and for permission to reproduce them:

Mrs. Dorothy Evans, for the postcards from her late husband's collection; Francis Frith Collection, plc.; Hampshire County Council Library and Museum Service; Mr. Bob Herbert; Mr. Douglas Lewis; the late Martin Loveridge Collection; Mr. Frank W. May; Mrs. Josephine Pay; Mr. John Penny; Mr. Arthur Rogers; Mrs. Marjorie Smith and Mr. Eric Wood. Others wished to remain anonymous.

Special thanks to Mr. John Marchment, not only for providing me with photographs, but for making copies of a number of postcards. I am grateful to Mr. Edwin Kendall, senior librarian at the Andover Library, for allowing me access to old street directories, photographs and local history publications. Few photographs or postcards bear a date, which makes it difficult for the researcher to be absolutely accurate. Early street directories were published at infrequent intervals and, whilst they provide the name of the existing business, they do not indicate when that business began or ended, so one can only give an approximate date. I am indebted to those persons, too numerous to name individually, who have provided information about events, shops and buildings mentioned in the captions.

Finally, grateful thanks to my daughter, Mrs. Sue Parker, for processing the script and captions.

Introduction

The name of Andover has a pre-Saxon source but there is no firm proof of when the town came into existence. It has been suggested that a settlement existed some 3,000 years ago.

The origin of the name is Celtic. The first part of the word Andover is the Gaelic An or Ean, meaning a spring; the second half is the Gaelic word Dufr, which means water – the early settlement being named from the springs which rise to the north of the town and from the river which runs through it, now called the Anton.

Gaelic Celts are known to have occupied this part of England earlier than 1500 B.C. The Romans were in the area for some 400 years but few traces of their occupation of the town have been found. They probably wanted to avoid the marshy area of the River Anton but some coins and tessellae or tiles (c.A.D.200) have been recovered from time to time. Yet the neighbourhood around has proved exceptionally rich in Roman pavements and the sites of villas and farm buildings. The Roman Icknield Way (Cirencester to Winchester) and Portway (Silchester to Old Sarum) crossed at Eastanton on the outskirts of the town.

First written records of communal life in Andover, or Andeferas as it was called, were made in Saxon times. The West Saxon kings had a residence in the town. King Edgar (943-75) held a Witengemot, or Saxon Parliament, here in 962. He often stayed at his Royal vill at Andover and hunted the vast forests of Chute and Harewood.

The year 994 was important in the history of Andover for that was when the Danes, under Sweyn, and the men of Norway, led by Olaf Tryggvason, were ravaging the south of England. They had burnt Romsey Abbey and King Olaf was guided by Alphege, Bishop of Winchester, to the Royal vill at Andover now occupied by King Ethelred (968-1016), a weak monarch who earned himself the name 'Ethelred the Unready'. Ethelred agreed to pay King Olaf the sum of £16,000 'Danegeld', as it was called, on condition that he became converted to Christianity and left the country for good. King Olaf agreed to the terms and was baptised by the Bishop of Winchester in the Saxon church at Andover. He kept his promise and left to rule Norway as its first Christian king.

Men from the Manor of Andover took part in the Battle of Hastings in 1066 but there is no record of the number involved. Under Norman rule the town was established as a Royal Manor and a new church was built. Originally dedicated to St Peter, it was a low solid building in which the townspeople worshipped for 700 years, until it was demolished in 1840. The present parish church of St Mary, which took its place, was completed in 1846. An arch from the west doorway of the old Norman church, dated c.1150, was saved and today stands in the upper part of the High Street, where it was erected in 1845.

In the disastrous civil war of 1141, at the time of King Stephen, Andover was practically burnt to the ground. Pursued by Royalists, the Empress Matilda, with 200 cavalry, was cornered here on her way from Winchester to Ludgershall Castle. She escaped and made her way to Devizes leaving a blazing town behind her. This was the first of three major conflagrations that devastated the town in its early history. Many houses, including the *College* Inn (*c*.1175), owned by Winchester College, were burnt out in a fire in 1435. Rebuilt in 1455, it was later renamed the *Angel*. Today it is the oldest of all the town's inns. Again, in 1647, many townspeople were made homeless when fire destroyed some 80 houses on low-lying land near the river.

The Merchant Guild of Andover was given its first charter by King Henry II in 1175. The fact that it granted the men of Andover a 'Guild of Merchants' showed that the town had developed from a manor at the time of Domesday to the status of a commercially important town. The bailiff and 24 forwardmen, comprising the guild, governed the town throughout the Middle Ages.

In 1201 King John granted the manor and town of Andover to the burgesses on payment of a fee-farm (rent) in return for which the bailiff, on behalf of the townspeople, received the manorial revenues. This charter was the first indication of the recognition of Andover as a town. Between 1355 and 1588 there were no less than 10 Royal charters defining the rights of the men of Andover.

Up until this period most of the town's development was on land between the river and the church, and the town's centre was probably in the vicinity of the *College* or *Angel* Inn. The borough archives contain early rental books giving some of the old street names. In the 1446 rental book, houses are described as being in Chepyngstreet, now the High Street. Frog Lane later became Soper's Street and, in more recent years, West Street. Now demolished, the street forms part of the town's new Chantry Shopping Centre complex.

Other old street names included Dog Pole Lane, known today as Church Hill or Marlborough Street; Wote Street is now London Street; Broadway, probably the old centre of Andover, later became London Lane and is now Vigo Road. White Lane and Back Lane were renamed East Street – now Eastern Avenue. Barlow's Lane was once known as Barber's Lane or Rolley's Lane. One of the few original names to remain is New Street. It was here that the men who built the town lived in their thatched cottages generation after generation.

The most important of all the town's charters was that granted by Queen Elizabeth I in 1599. It made Andover a 'free borough' and a 'body corporate and politic', and resulted in the government of the town being vested in a high steward, recorder, town clerk, 12 approved men and 12 capital burgesses. There were also a bailiff and two magistrates. The bailiff had the right to appoint two sergeants-at-mace to attend him. In addition to the magistrates' courts, to be held when necessary, a court of quarter sessions was granted for the borough, together with a court of record (county court), for debts and damages under £40, to be held every Monday.

Andover was the centre of jurisdiction for the town and district from early days, courts being held every Monday for, alternately, the In-and-Out Hundreds. These courts were granted by King John in his charter of 1213 and they were presided over by the Bailiff of Andover. The In-Hundred consisted of the tithings of Alderman-le-Grand (an area including the upper part of Andover's High Street, the priory, an area around the church and Winchester Street, which also included the lower High Street and part of Bridge Street), Enhan Regis, Charlton and Hatherden.

The tithingmen came to the court of Out-Hundred from the parishes of Abbotts Ann, Amport, Cholderton and Appleshaw, Upper Clatford, Fyfiels, Grately, Kimpton and Littleton, Knights Enham, Penton Mewsey, Thruxton, South Tisworth and Penton Grafton (Weyhill). The court entries, in the main, refer to pleas concerning debt, land, transgressions, trespass, theft, and assault and battery. Debtors, for example, usually ended up in the town's prison and many culprits no doubt experienced the discomfort of the stocks or pillory which were located outside the Town Hall!

In addition, the ancient courts of Frank Pledge, Court Leet and Manor Court were held. By the Charter of 1599 the old Hundred Court was superseded by a Court of Record held every Monday, in the Guildhall, before the bailiff or his deputy.

The terms of the 1599 charter came to an end with the passing of the Municipal Corporation Act of 1835 and from then until 1974 the town council, headed by a mayor, four aldermen and 12 councillors together with a town clerk and a recorder, looked after Andover's interests. The first town mayor to be appointed in 1836 was Robert Dowling. In 1974 Andover lost its borough status and became part of the much larger Test Valley Borough Council.

In 1295, and from 1302 to 1307, Andover returned two members of Parliament. In 1311 writs were received but it appears no-one in the town was prepared to serve as an M.P., probably due to the expense and what was at that time a dangerous journey to London, and so Andover was not represented again until 1586. From that year onwards two members were sent regularly but in 1867, under the Representation of the People Act, the number was reduced to one. In 1885 Andover ceased to be a parliamentary division in its own right and became part of a larger constituency in north-west Hampshire, the name of the constituency changing several times over the years.

How did Andover survive those early years? There were many small farms on its perimeter supplying the townspeople with food and, in the town, cloth-making was the principal industry offering employment. In 1272 one of the chief traders, Alexander the Rich, was permitted to export 44 sacks of wool and the following year a licence was granted to five Andover merchants to export 124 sacks of wool. The trade flourished well into the 17th century. Fleeces were sold at an annual fair in June until the early part of this century.

There was an iron market at Andover in the 14th century and when, in 1471, the bells of the parish church needed restoring, local ironworkers carried out the task. Other important industries were lime-burning, tanning and parchment-making – the town supplying parchment to the Royal Chancery at an early date. At the end of the Close Roll for 1228, now in the Public Record Office, there is a note in Latin which reads: 'Six dozen parchments from Andevere, price four pence per dozen'.

On the demise of the wool trade Andover became noted for producing silk and shalloons (a light woollen cloth). There was a large silk factory just off the present Eastfield Road.

During the years 1603-5, 1625-6 and 1636 Andover's population was substantially reduced by the plague and it is recorded that the town and surrounding area 'suffered greatly'. The Andover parish registers for those years reveal that the plague first reached the town on 10 August 1603. Several hundred people died during this period with whole families being wiped out. In June 1605, for example, an entry in the register read: 'William, son of Richard Pilgram; Richard Pilgram and Joyce, his daughter, his other daughter (no name given)'. Richard Pilgram's wife and another child had died a year earlier.

Andover changed hands many times during the Civil War. The Royalist garrison from Winchester often raided the town and on one occasion took away £10,000-worth of cloth from the townspeople, some indication of the town's prosperity during that period. Several local men took part in the abortive 'rising in the West' against Cromwell's forces. Two of them were later hanged at Exeter for their part in the rebellion.

In 1643 a group of people left the town for the 'New World' and there founded the town's namesake in Massachusetts. Visits between the two towns have taken place in recent years. When, in 1653, Admiral Blake defeated the Dutch Admiral, Van Tromp, taking a large number of prisoners, about fifty of these prisoners were brought to Andover. Some were lodged in the town's gaol by the river in Bridge Street. During the Seven Years War, on the continent from 1756-63, a large number of French prisoners were taken and about a hundred of these were housed in the town. Most of them were kept in barns at the back of some of the town's inns. The parish register for 1758 records that three prisoners were buried in the churchyard at St Mary's on 4, 7 and 29 October respectively. French officers were allowed parole and were billeted on families in the town and district. Again, the parish registers show that at least three of these officers married local girls and took their wives back to France when hostilities ceased. More French prisoners were brought here during the period of the Napoleonic War, 1793-1802. French gentry who escaped from France at the time were also living in the town. One such refugee was a 26-year-old teacher named François Lirochons. Whilst here he fell in love with an Andover girl of his own age but she spurned that love and he shot himself. He was buried in St Mary's churchyard and the entry in the parish register for 13 September 1793 reads: 'François Lirochons, aged 26 years, was buried. (A gent from France, who, in a fit of lunacy, shot himself.)'.

It was towards the end of the 18th century that major changes began to take place. In 1785 Andover's large, open fields were enclosed by the Andover Enclosure Award and the Ladies' Walk was laid down for use of all the townspeople. The walk, on high ground to the east and south of the town, even today offers excellent views of the sprawling borough.

The year 1789 saw the opening of the Andover canal, an important route from the town to Southampton. Twenty-two miles long, it started just off Bridge Street (where Safeway's food store stands today) and ran to the tideway at Redbridge, on the outskirts of Southampton. Several hundred navvies were employed to dig out the canal using just picks and shovels, for there were no mechanical aids in those days. It had a fall to sea level of 179 ft. and was aided by 24 locks on its route. The total cost was £48,000, made up of £35,000 in shares and £13,000 of loan note. The barges carried coal, building materials, fish and other goods from Southampton to Romsey, Stockbridge and Andover, and on the return journey mainly agricultural produce was transported. The stone used in building St Mary's church during the period 1842-6 was brought up by barge after having been shipped to Southampton from Normandy. Unfortunately the trade was not enough to earn a dividend for its proprietors and the canal was closed in September 1859. It was filled in and a railway, built on some 14½ miles of its route, was opened in 1865. The line was affectionately known as the 'Sprat and Winkle' line, a nickname which arose from the fact that the barges which used the canal would often bring up baskets of sprats and winkles to the town. Jars of illegal brandy would be smuggled in the bottom of these baskets, as it was thought that the strong smell would put the customs officers off searching through them. The line was eventually axed by Lord Beeching in 1964 after being in existence for just 99 years.

Notes in a local directory of 1792 show that there was still a large proportion of thatched dwellings in the town, including the High Street. A small stream trickled across the market place from Wakeford's bank to the covered way next to Waterloo House. 'There were no policemen nor perambulators, no pavements nor gas lamps ... sedan chairs were still in use but more people were to be seen on horseback.' The stocks were situated in the Guildhall forecourt and were often used. The grammar school stood opposite the Vicarage and there was a theatre on the right-hand side of Newbury Street, with accommodation consisting of 'a gallery, pit, slips and boxes'. It closed in the 1830s. The Ladies' Walk had been established – 'the sole playground of the town, though prize fights and such-like gentle entertainments were occasionally given in the ground opposite the *Queen Charlotte* Inn in London Road'.

The 19th century saw tremendous strides in the development of the town. The Paving, Lighting and Cleansing Act for Andover was passed in 1815. The town's gasworks was constructed in 1838 just three years after the passing of the Municipal Corporation Act which changed the structure of local government in the town (as mentioned above). The railway line from London to Andover was opened in 1854 and extended to Salisbury in 1857. It was the opening of this line that brought an end to the town's thriving coaching business and for a time caused considerable hardship to innkeepers and shopkeepers. Coaches and waggons passed through the town regularly in the second half of the 18th century but when Pitt, the Prime Minister, agreed to proposals to run regular mail coaches throughout the country in 1784, local business increased three-fold. Over 30 coaches a day were passing through Andover as well as numerous waggons carrying goods. Most of the coaches would make a stop to change horses and enable passengers to refresh themselves. Coaches using the route from London to the West Country included the 'Exeter Balloon Coach', 'Steadman's Light Salisbury Coach', 'The London and Taunton Coach' and Cooke's coach from Salisbury. Coaches travelling from Southampton to Oxford also called in at Andover. The town was kept busy day and night coping with the trade.

The population of the town in 1861 was 5,221 and the numbers grew steadily to the turn of the century. Brewing was of some importance in the 1800s and there were two or three large breweries in the town. The main ones were Heath's (started in 1778), Colcock's – later Hammans (1878) – controlling at least 14 tied public houses, Poore's and Nutley's. In the 1860s there were 38 hotels, inns and beer houses within the borough boundary.

The general pattern of employment in Andover was beginning to change in the mid-19th century. Men and boys were drifting away from agriculture to work in the building trade which was beginning to expand. Land to the west of the River Anton was being developed rapidly as new houses were built in Junction Road, Weyhill Road, Salisbury Road and Millway Road. More homes were to follow in these areas by the turn of the century. Several light engineering works were being established, which called for skilled tradesmen. The largest of these firms was Taskers, started in 1815, with a factory on the outskirts of the town at Anna Valley. By the 1880s well over 100 men and boys were employed in manufacturing agricultural machinery, such as ploughs, drills and steam traction engines. In the 1890s men were leaving the town to travel daily to nearby Tidworth to work on building a new Army garrison – barracks, parade grounds and hundreds of homes. Similarly a large number of local tradesmen helped to build the air force station opened at Andover in 1916.

Religion has played its part in the progress of the town throughout the centuries. The present Anglican parish church of St Mary, built on high ground at the top of the High Street, replaced the old Norman church on that site in 1846. A handsome and spacious building, it is a fine example of early Victorian Gothic architecture and can seat up to 1,000 people. The church tower dominates the whole town and it is a landmark for miles around. The £30,000 required to build St Mary's was provided by the late Reverend W. Stanley Goddard, D.D., who was a former headmaster of Winchester College. On resigning from that post in 1809 he came to live at Andover in the house which he, in 1845, bequeathed to become the vicarage. The poor of the town have benefited over the years from the various charities vested in the church.

The Andover Congregational Church, or Independent Chapel as it was called, lies just off the Eastern distributor road. It was formed in 1662 and the present chapel, built in 1700 with seating for over 600 people, is now the oldest church building in the town. A Baptist Church was founded in Andover on 12 January 1824 and the following year a chapel was built. It was replaced by a larger chapel in the upper High Street in 1866 at a cost of £1,800. The building was demolished in 1981 on completion of a new church in Charlton Road.

Methodism came to Andover in the mid-18th century. On 7 November 1790 John Wesley wrote: 'I preached about nine at Andover to a few dead stones'. It was during the ministry of John Haime at Whitchurch (1744-84) that Andover Methodists acquired a chapel. Andover Circuit records date from 1818 when the circuit had 13 societies with a total membership of 204. In 1824 a new church was built in Brick Kiln Street (now Winchester Street) at a cost of £1,050. The Wesleyans occupied the building until moving to their present church in Bridge Street, which cost nearly £4,000 in 1906. The premises they vacated were taken over by the Andover Corps, No. 637, of the Salvation Army which had established itself in the town in 1858. In 1838 the Primitive Methodists built a chapel in East Street but the building was demolished in the 1960s to make way for the new inner ring road. Another Methodist Church was opened in Weyhill Road in 1956, not far from the Anglican parish church of St Michael and All Angels, established in 1951.

The Roman Catholic Church had a small building in Weyhill Road before a new church building, dedicated to St John the Baptist, was built in Alexandra Road in 1956. There are a number of other religious bodies in the town for different beliefs.

Little is left today of the older part of the centre of Andover, now a conservation area, but there is one building which remains aloof in the High Street – the Guildhall. The present structure was erected in 1825 at a cost of £7,000, replacing the one which had stood on the site since 1742. Early records show that there had been a 'town house' in Andover since 1582. Now the Guildhall has lost much of its status for no longer are the magistrates' courts, quarter sessions and county court held within its walls. The corn exchange on the ground floor also ceased in the 1970s at the same time as the courts. More recently several of the Test Valley Borough Council meetings, which had been held in the council chamber on the first floor, have been transferred to the borough's new £6-million headquarters at Beech Hurst in Weyhill Road.

Today Andover, with a population of over 32,000, has a thriving community and offers a wide variety of industry on two large industrial estates, prime office accommodation and a modern town centre including a covered shopping complex.

It is left to the early photographers of yesteryear to portray the town's past glories in the plates which are to follow.

The first recorded professional photographer in Andover was Frederic Pearse, who opened a studio adjoining the Post Office in the High Street in 1868 or 1869. At the time the town's population was a little over 5,000 and it was not a particularly prosperous period. An advertisement in a local trade directory of 1870 announcing Mr. Pearse's arrival read: 'Mr. Pearse has recently opened a capacious and well-fitted photographic studio ... the very favourable locale of which enables him to produce portraits in every style of the highest excellence without reference to the existing state of the weather'. He

1. Studio portrait of an unnamed lady by Frederic Pearse, portrait and landscape photographer, *c.*1872.

2. A fine head and shoulders portrait by Charles Howard, *c.*1895.

3. Walter Herbert, son of Charles Herbert, farmer of Eastanton, near Andover, aged 21. The portrait was taken by Henry Partridge, of Union Street, in 1890.

4. A well-posed studio portrait by F. Browne, of Browne and Gradidge, chemists and photographic suppliers in the High Street, c.1890.

changed premises later; *White's Directory* of Hampshire for 1896 lists his studio as being at 9 and 11 Winchester Street.

In 1899 he was back in the High Street at No. 63 with a business known as The Andover Bazaar described as 'a fancy repository and toys'. His studio was at the rear of the shop. The photographic side of the business appears to have ceased by the early 1920s and the family concentrated on selling toys, for which it was renowned throughout the town and district. The shop was closed in the early 1970s.

Mr. Pearse was a man of high principles and was much respected in the town. He fought compulsory vaccination and refused to have any of his children vaccinated. He appeared in court over 60 times during the 1890s, being forced to pay fines totalling over £40. But on Wednesday, 11 February 1897 the magistrates' patience ran out and he was sent to prison for three days in default of paying the costs of his 63rd prosecution as he had '... no goods, stock or furniture to distrain on, it all being his wife's'. When he was released from prison three days later hundreds of people were at the town station to welcome him home. Headed by a brass band, a procession, with Mr. Pearse at its head, made its way to the Guildhall where a public protest meeting was staged. The hall was packed and hundreds more stood outside – such was the feeling about vaccination in Andover at that time.

In the early 1880s Charles Howard opened a studio in London Street concentrating initially on taking portraits and family groups. At the time he described himself as a 'photo artist and picture framer under distinguished patronage'. He built his own plate camera – as did many professional photographers in those days – to enable him to start in business. By 1895 he had moved to premises in the upper High Street at No. 81 and had widened the scope of his activities to include photographing current events in the life of the town. His services were much sought after, particularly at official civic functions, for his work was of a high standard. By the mid-1920s one of his daughters, Edith Howard, had joined the family business which moved to premises on the opposite side of the street, No. 74, in 1933. Her brother, Charles, and her sister ran a similar photographic business at Eastgate Square, Chichester, under the family name. It ceased trading in the early 1980s. Edith Howard disposed of the Andover shop to Mr. R. Page, ARPS, in 1957. Mr. Page was the first professional photographer in the town to produce a colour print of a wedding group in 1958. Although he retired in 1986 the firm of Howard's, Photographers, still trades from the same premises but under different proprietors.

Joining Pearse and Howard in the town around the early 1880s was Henry Simonds Partridge who opened a studio in Union Street close to where Pearse had started. By 1895 he had also moved into the upper High Street at No. 73. Besides studio work he covered outdoor events producing many pictures in postcard format. He ceased business in the town at the turn of the century.

A long-established firm in Andover was Browne and Gradidge Ltd., dispensing and photographic chemists, whose premises were at Jubilee House in the lower High Street. In the 1870s the firm was known as Gradidge and Son but when the son, William Ivimey Gradidge, married the daughter of Mr. Frederick Browne, a publisher, the title of the firm was changed to Browne and Gradidge. A photographic studio was added to the premises in the 1880s. The firm also joined other photographers in recording outside activities and published postcards depicting street scenes in the town and district. The studio closed in the early 1920s but a chemist's shop was on the site until the 1970s.

The most prolific of all the town's early photographers was Fred Wright. He was at the scene of most events in the town and district in the period from 1905 to the early

1920s when he sold up and opened another business at Southsea. Mr. Wright had a small studio in the village of Shipton Bellinger, near Andover, at the turn of the century. From there he would cycle to the nearby Tidworth Army Garrison to take pictures of soldiers at the barracks. He photographed hundreds of troops over the next few years before moving, in 1905, to 73a High Street, Andover, vacated by photographer Henry Partridge. Nearly fifty per cent of old postcards in collectors' hands today were taken by him. His name always appeared at the bottom left- or right-hand corner of a postcard. On occasions he supplied pictures of local major incidents – train and plane crashes, etc. – to the national newspapers. His wife played an important rôle in the business, for it was she who did the bulk of the developing and printing and took portraits in the studio. For a period after World War One, Mr. Wright frequently returned to Tidworth Garrison to take shots of groups of soldiers but, by this time, he had a motorcycle combination in which to transport his camera equipment. The Wrights had three sons and a daughter. The eldest son, Lionel, followed in his father's footsteps by joining a photographic firm in Southampton.

A popular 'travelling' photographer of this same period was Mr. Sam Taylor. Known as 'the last plate man' he used to cycle around the area taking shots of groups of people and calling on homes offering to take family portraits. He did not use a studio but had a darkroom at his home in Chantry Street where he did all his developing and printing, delivering the finished pictures himself. There are still many postcards in existence bearing the name 'Sam Taylor' scratched in the left-hand corner.

George Wheaton commenced his photographic business at 61 Junction Road in about 1912. His studio darkroom was in a wooden shed at the side of his home. Besides portrait work he also concentrated on outdoor events. His series of pictures of the 1916 rail crash at Andover Junction Station were particularly noteworthy. A local directory showed him still in business in 1923 but he seems to have disappeared after that date.

5.   A group of wounded soldiers with some of their nurses at Rothsay House, near Andover, taken by Fred Wright, *c.*1915.

6. War-time workers at Taskers' Waterloo Iron Works, photographed by Sam Taylor, 1915.

When the Post Office legalised the use of postcards in 1894, some of the larger commercial firms sent photographers around the country taking views of street scenes and popular beauty spots. F. Frith and Company Limited became a major supplier of postcards and regularly visited Andover over the years. A large number of cards in local collectors' hands bear the name 'F. Frith and Co. Ltd., Reigate' and today the Francis Frith Collection, which is now under the guidance of Mr. John Buck, is housed at Andover.

Another well-known postcard supplier of Andover scenes until about 1910 was Whitfield Cosser of Southampton and Salisbury. Several shops in the town sold postcards, offered to them by the commercial companies, bearing the name of their premises as publishers. These included Holmes and Sons, L. Mair, S. Rolls, W. Portsmouth and Weaver and Co. to name just a few.

Bibliography

Bennett, Arthur C., *Things Passed Away*, 1918
Berry, C. J. J., *Old Andover*, 1976
Earney, H. W., *Inns of Andover*, 1955
Longstaff, Stella M., *Andover Grammar School 1569-1951*, 1951
Paintin, Bernard R. K., *Since Wesley Came to Andover*, 1951
Parsons, Edmund, *Notes on the History of Andover*, 1921
Spaul, John, *Andover*, 1977
Files of the *Andover Advertiser*

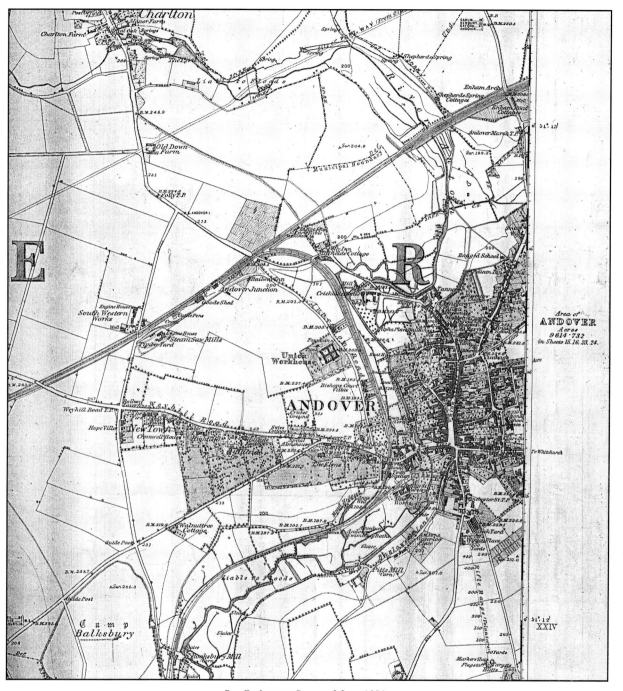

7. Ordnance Survey Map, 1871.

8.　The upper High Street in the late 1870s. A young apprentice outside W. G. Hayes' linen shop pauses for the photographer whilst engaged in hanging out a display of stock. Standing in front of the covered wagon on the right is Mr. Luke Bull, senior, a chimney sweep who lived in New Street.

9.　Three little girls with a younger child walking along the High Street, *c.*1896. On the left is 3 High Street, the offices of the *Andover Standard*. This weekly newspaper ceased publication in 1900. Directly opposite are the offices of the rival weekly newspaper, the *Andover Advertiser*, still occupying the same site today.

10. The Palladian-style Guildhall in 1898. The clock tower was removed in 1904 because its weight was too great and it was sinking into the roof. The clock from the tower was fitted within the gable.

11. On 6 July 1893 the town celebrated the wedding of the Duke and Duchess of York – the late King George V and Queen Mary – with a procession through the town centre. The banners of local friendly societies are prominent in the foreground.

12. Queen Victoria's Diamond Jubilee was celebrated with an open-air dinner in the High Street in 1897. Around 3,500 people sat down to a meal at tables laid on either side of the wide street. All the shops were decorated and many bore suitable greetings: 'God bless Victoria 1837-1897', 'A Reign of Prosperity' or 'She Wrought Her People Lasting Good'. The picture was taken by Frederic Pearse from one of the first floor windows of the Guildhall.

13. Before the Diamond Jubilee celebration dinner there was a grand procession which had to wend its way between the tables on either side of the High Street.

14.   Some of the people who sat down to enjoy the meal.

15.   On Wednesday, 9 July 1897 the 3rd Dragoon Guards and the Scots Greys paraded in the High Street. The units, on their way from Aldershot to Salisbury Plain, were accorded a civic reception.

16. Workmen engaged in laying a main sewer in the upper High Street, *c*.1900. On the immediate left is Buckland's and then Cocking's jewellers' premises. The protruding sign of 'F. Pearse, Photographer' can be seen, with the larger wording, 'The Andover Bazaar, F. Pearse', higher up on the side of the shop. It remained a toy shop until the early 1970s, when it was lost under the redevelopment scheme.

17. A view of the upper High Street, 1898. The building on the left – 51 High Street – was at one time the offices of Poore's brewery and later became Scott's shoe shop. It was demolished in the late 1960s to make way for the new shopping centre. The taller building just visible on the right is the Andover Baptist church, which was pulled down in 1981 and replaced by shops.

18. The year 1902 saw more celebrations in the town with the Coronation of King Edward VII. The activities included a procession of horse-drawn tableaux through the High Street. The event was marred by rain as the host of umbrellas indicates.

19. Included in the procession were the town's stocks. The man with the beard seated in the stocks was a well-known local character, Mr. 'Spud' Yates, who had the unique distinction of being the last person to occupy them during the reign of Queen Victoria.

20. Looking at the front of the *Angel* Inn, upper High Street, from Newbury Street, *c.*1898. Originally the *College* Inn, dating back to 1175, it was once the property of Winchester College. The inn was destroyed by fire in 1435 but the college authorities were not able to rebuild it until 1445. Richard Pope, the poet, held the lease in 1582. By this time it had been renamed the *Angel*, and is now the oldest inn in the town.

A. B. SCOTT,

Fashionable Bootmaker,

74, High Street, ANDOVER.

21. Mr. A. B. Scott's shoe shop at 74 High Street, *c.*1909 – now Howard's, the photographers – before he moved to 51 High Street. Locals called the area 'Scott's corner' until the shop was demolished.

22. Just above Scott's corner at 55, 57 and 59 High Street were
L. Buckland and Son, drapers and outfitters, pictured here
c.1906. The firm was started by Mr. Laude Buckland in the late
1860s. Buckland's closed just after World War Two.

23. This advertisement, published in a local directory in 1909,
shows Mr. F. W. Rogers standing in the doorway of his shop at
58 High Street. He gave up the business in 1914 or 1915.

24.   The top of the upper High Street, *c*.1906. Most of the buildings in front of St Mary's church remain intact today, although the shop fronts have been changed.

25. Mr. Maurice Crang, who took over the shop from Mr. Rogers. He occupied the premises until 1937 when the site was sold to Marks and Spencer. They built a new store, which was opened in 1938 and is still there today. Mr. Crang moved down the street to No. 46 and opened another ironmonger's shop. It was closed in 1953 and is now Samuel's, the jewellers.

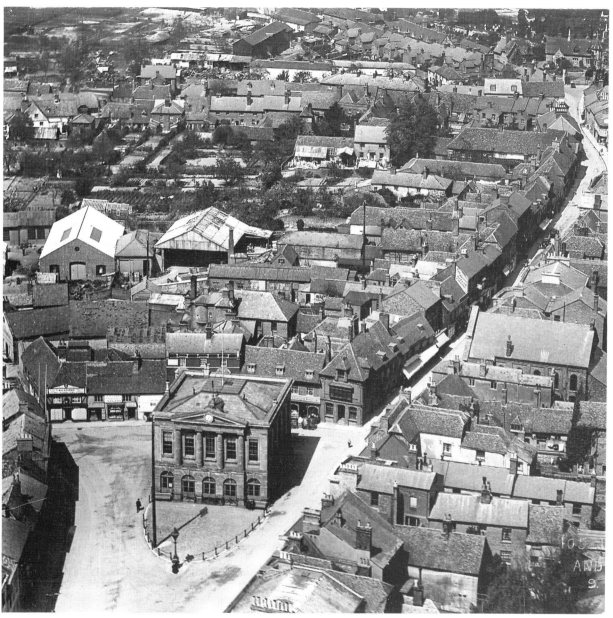

26.   One of the first aerial views of Andover's town centre. It was taken on 5 May 1918, just after the establishment of an aerial photographic unit at R.A.F. Andover. Virtually all the buildings directly behind the Guildhall were demolished in the late 1960s to make way for the Chantry Shopping Centre and the redevelopment of part of the upper High Street.

27.   High Street under snow, 25 April 1908. The mayor (Alderman Thomas Webb) arranged for the unemployed to shovel the snow off the pavements, for the convenience of the townspeople.

28. The demolition of the beautiful old St Mary's church in the early 1840s was a source of regret to many Andoverians at the time. The £30,000 required to build the new church, completed in 1846, was provided by the Rev. W. Stanley Goddard, D.D., who was formerly headmaster of Winchester College.

29. All that remains of the old Norman church is this arch (*c.*1150) which was re-erected in the upper High Street in 1845. The arch originally formed the west doorway of the old building.

30. St Mary's parish church viewed from a southerly aspect, *c*.1898. All the tombstones in the foreground were removed
to form a Garden of Remembrance in 1956.

31. The church seen from the north, *c*.1898. The foreground shows the graveyard where most of the early burials took place.

32. The interior of St Mary's taken by one of Francis Frith's photographers at the turn of the century.

33.   Another aerial view of Andover in 1918. The long road in the foreground is Old Winton Road. Just to the left is part of Andover golf course and Winchester Road. The fields on the right behind St Mary's church were developed from the late 1960s under the town's overspill programme. In the extreme top left of the picture can be seen part of the track of the old 'Sprat and Winkle' railway line, which ran from Andover Junction to Southampton.

34. The top half of Old Winton Road, seen in the aerial photograph, taken about ten years earlier.

35. Local farmers bidding for a ram, at an auction in front of the Guildhall, *c.*1898. The annual sale of rams – mostly Hampshire Down – was a popular event with the farming community. The sales ended in the late 1930s.

36.   Workmen handling bales of fleeces at the Walled Meadow, *c.*1902. For centuries the annual wool sale was held every June, but it came to an end in the mid-1930s.

The Swimming Baths, Adelaide Road, ANDOVER

OPEN FROM MAY TO OCTOBER.

PRIVATE HOT & COLD BATHS DAILY FROM MAY TO OCTOBER, AND SATURDAYS ONLY FROM NOVEMBER TO APRIL.

F. BEALE, Proprietor.

37. Adelaide Road, *c.*1900. On the left is the *Adelaide Tavern*, formerly the *Carpenters Arms*, and renamed the *Lardicake* in 1974. The landlord for many years during the 19th century was George Curtis, who became mayor of Andover in 1880. On the right was the town's first heated indoor swimming pool, built in 1885. The baths were open from May to October but in the winter months the bath was covered and the building became the Assembly Rooms. It was used for various entertainments and meetings. Closed in the 1920s, it was for many years a furniture store before being demolished in 1975, to make way for the Adelaide Medical Centre and a block of flats.

38. An advertisement for the Assembly Rooms which appeared in a local trade directory in 1909.

39. Eastfield Road, *c*.1898, leading off Recreation Road. The chalk and thatched cottages have long since disappeared, but the brick and slate row of houses on the extreme left of the picture remain. They have been refurbished over the years.

40. Eastfield Road at its junction with East Street, *c*.1902. The large building with the tall chimney in the background was Hammans brewery. It became a chicken hatchery in the early 1920s and then the Andover Family Laundry. The building was demolished in the 1960s to make way for a car park. Behind the little girl, to the left, is the old Andover Fire Station.

41.   The *Spotted Dog* public house, East Street, pictured here in the 1890s, when it was owned by
Hammans. It stood almost opposite the brewery and was later taken over by Strong and Co. Ltd. of
Romsey who, until 1926, had a brewery at Weyhill, near Andover. It was pulled down in 1969 to make
way for the Eastern distributor road.

42.   Henry Hammans, the brewer, controlled a dozen or more public
houses in the area from c.1880 until the turn of the century. He also owned
four licensed liquor stores in the town – at East Street, London Street, New
Street and Bridge Street. Note the 1902-3 prices of the beer!

W. O. NUTLEY,

PHŒNIX BREWERY,

(YE OLD CHANTRY)

ANDOVER.

BITTER, MILD, STRONG, AND OLD ALES, BREWED FROM BEST ENGLISH MALT AND HOPS ONLY.

Agent for Barclay & Perkin's Celebrated London Stout.

DELIVERED FREE WITHIN A RADIUS OF 50 MILES.

43.   This advertisement for W. O. Nutley's Phœnix brewery appeared in 1898. The brewery was beside the *Phoenix Inn* in Chantry Street, which dates back to 1636. In 1864 Charles Nutley, a maltster of Hurstbourne Tarrant, and William Nutley, a common brewer of Newbury, bought a property next to the *Phoenix* and started brewing. The brewery went out of business in the early 1920s, but a member of the Nutley family ran the *Phoenix* until 1926. The building was demolished in the 1960s.

44.   East Street, *c.*1902. All the properties on the left were demolished in the late 1960s to make way for Eastern Avenue. The elegant houses on the right have been converted into prestige office accommodation.

45. To the right is the Andover Congregational church (*c.*1919-20) in what used to be East Street. Built in 1700 it is the oldest church building in the town. The church now fronts the new distributor road. In the cottage on the right, pulled down in the 1960s, lived a well-known character called Luke Bull, jun., a chimney sweep. The wording on the board above the front door read: 'Luke Bull lives here, attends to orders far and near. With his brush, scraper and machine he will sweep your chimney clean. And, if it should ever catch fire, he will put it out at your desire'.

46. These ladies are enjoying a rest in the pleasant surroundings of the Vigo Road Recreation Ground, *c.*1906. To the left of the trees is the Common Acre where the town's bowmen used to practise their archery. At the far end of the path lie the former Acre Almshouses and the *Borough Arms* public house.

47.   Children playing cricket in another part of the Vigo Road Recreation Ground, *c*.1912. St Mary's parish church can be seen in the background.

48. Customers sitting on beer barrels outside the *Borough Arms* Inn opposite the Common Acre, *c*.1900. The inn, built in the 1860s, was called the *Andover Arms* until 1878. The outward appearance of the building has changed little over the intervening years.

ANDOVER.

FREEHOLD
PROPERTY.

TO BE

Sold by Auction,

BY

R. DREW,

On FRIDAY, the 19th of JUNE, 1835,

AT SEVEN O'CLOCK IN THE EVENING,

AT THE GEORGE INN, ANDOVER,

THE FOLLOWING

FREEHOLD
PROPERTY.

Lot 1. ALL that Substantial Brick Built and Thatched TENE-
MENT or DWELLING HOUSE, situate in the Acre,
in Andover, now in the occupation of Mr. HENDY,
Tenant at will, at the low Yearly Rent of £7.

Lot 2. All those newly erected DWELLING HOUSES, substantially Brick built with Stuccoed Fronts and Slated
Roofs, all attached, and adjoining Lot 1, now in the
Occupation of Responsible Tenants, at the low clear
annual Rent of £20. 12.

May be viewed on application to the respective Tenants,
and further particulars known from the Auctioneer, and of Mr.
MANN, Solicitor, Andover.

BENSLEY, PRINTER, ANDOVER.

49. Notice of sale of freehold property at the *George* Inn (Hotel), High Street, in June 1835. Fronting the Common Acre, the houses were ideally situated. Lot 2 consisted of six new homes which were occupied for 140 years before being demolished in the mid-1970s and replaced by a block of flats. The single house had a similar fate.

50.   The *George* Hotel, *c*.1902, just off the High Street, dates back to around 1586. Early records show that it existed in 1639. In the 18th and 19th centuries it was a prominent coaching stage-post and had a large range of stabling.

51. High Street, *c*.1898. All the shops appear closed, and the well-dressed people on the pavements and in the roadway indicate that the photograph was taken on a Sunday. The alley leading to the *George* Hotel can be seen just below Pouncey's shop on the right.

52. An early sketch of the High Street, *c*.1838-9. The Guildhall was built in 1825 and is the building just behind on the right (Scott's corner) in 1835. The Norman church seen in the background was not replaced until 1846. On the immediate right the structure of the *Star and Garter* Hotel (now the *Danebury* Hotel) has hardly altered.

53. The Tedworth Hunt assembling outside the Guildhall in 1912 prior to moving off to hunt the fields and woods to the west of the town. The kennels for the 30 couples of foxhounds was at Tidworth. The original pack was founded by the late Thomas Assheton-Smith, of Tidworth House, in about 1828.

54.   Shaw and Son's grocer's shop at 9 High Street, *c.*1904. Started by Miriam Shaw, a widow from Newbury, in 1808, it remained in the family until 1913. It was then purchased by Marcus Carter who continued trading under the name of Shaw's. Three generations of the Carter family ran the business until it closed in 1988.

55.   Browne and Gradidge's premises in the High Street, *c.*1909.

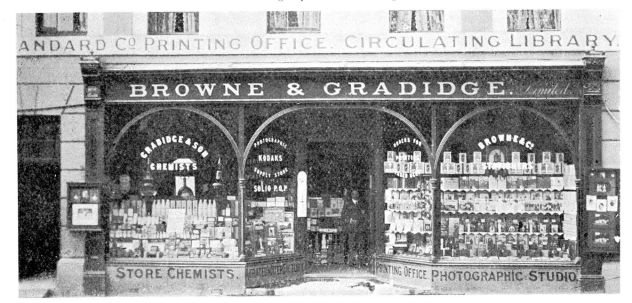

56. Parsons and Hart, High Street, *c.*1909. The firm Parsons and Sons was founded in 1839. In the 1870s Mr. Hart joined the partnership and the name was changed. The departmental store was the largest in the town, selling a wide range of stock. In the 1960s it became part of the Army and Navy group of stores for a short time before it was sold and demolished. Woolworth and two other shops were built on the site in the early 1970s.

57. This splendid steam waggon was used by Parsons and Hart for deliveries and furniture removals at the turn of the century.

58. The *Chequers* Hotel, High Street, *c.*1903-4. Known in later years as the *Rose and Chequers* it was a popular meeting place for farmers attending the weekly corn exchange at the Guildhall on a Friday, as it was granted an extension on its licence in the afternoon! A popular landlord at the turn of the century was John Culling, an excellent chef and caterer. Mr. Culling was also a keen dancer and at the back of the hotel he built the Waverley Hall which staged small dances, with a live band, for many years. He died in 1946. After the last war the hall housed the Ministry of Social Security and is now a photographic studio. The *Rose and Chequers* was pulled down in 1970 and the site is now occupied by Halfords.

59. The Andover Sunday School Union procession passing along the High Street in 1906. Note the splendid banner, showing that the union was established in 1872.

60. Another part of the lengthy procession, including the Salvation Army band. Similar displays of Christian unity were a regular feature of town life at the turn of the century.

61. The Andover Corps of the Salvation Army – No. 637 – was formed in 1884, and by the following year had established its own band. Outside a cottage in New Street, where the corps first met, are some of those early bandsmen including F. Sims, Fred Hendy, F. Cook, Dick Paris, A. Webb, Tommy Tubb, A. Paris and Freddie Hughes.

62. Members of the Andover Corps of the Salvation Army, accompanied by the band, parade along South Street in 1920 prior to Sunday morning service at the Winchester Street Citadel. The officer in charge, Ensign Benest, is on the extreme right.

63. Salvationists W. Latimer (left) and J. Silvert standing by a display of fruit, flowers and vegetables which they had arranged for the Andover Corps' harvest festival in the Foresters Hall, London Street, in 1902.

64. Standing outside the *Star and Garter* Hotel in the High Street is Mr. W. J. Randall's bus, the first double-decker motor bus to be seen in the town. It was purchased from a firm at Guildford, and had seating for 32 passengers with plenty of room for luggage.

65. The timetable for the town's first motor bus service, which was started in May 1906 by Mr. Randall, proprietor of the Andover Motor Omnibus Company. The route covered was from Andover to Tidworth Barracks and back. Unfortunately the fares were higher than those charged by the railway, so few people used the bus. Despite cutting his fares Mr. Randall was unable to make the service pay, and it came to an end in mid-July after being in operation for just 10 weeks.

T.A.N. SYNDICATE LTD.,

—— MOTOR GARAGE, ——

—— ANDOVER. ——

66. In 1911 the T.A.N. Syndicate Ltd. opened a garage at the Repository in Bridge Street. Besides hiring out cars and motor omnibuses for outings, the company also revived the ill-fated bus service between Andover and Tidworth. By this time the rail fares had increased and people found it cheaper and more convenient to use the buses, so T.A.N. were in business for at least four years.

67. A church parade passes along the High Street to celebrate the Coronation of King George V in 1911. The shops of Fry and Sons and A. W. Barton, seen in the background, were demolished in 1931 to be replaced by F. W. Woolworth's first store in the town. The Midland Bank now occupies this site, for Woolworth's moved across the street to a new store in the early 1970s.

68. In pouring rain, the procession to mark the Coronation of King George V in 1911 wends its way along Bridge Street. The foreground shows the manual hand pump used by the town's fire brigade in the mid-1800s.

69.   New Street, looking up towards Newbury Street, *c*.1898. The building on the left with the lamp outside was the old *Elephant* Inn. The thatched cottages on the immediate left were part of a row destroyed by fire in 1936. All the buildings seen in the picture have now gone.

70. Looking down New Street towards Enham Arch, *c.*1900.

71. On Easter Monday, 9 April 1901, a fire in New Street destroyed farm buildings, the *Blacksmith's Arms* public house and 17 cottages. Nearly 100 people, many of them children, were made homeless and lost all their possessions. A town collection raised £124 in just one day to help the fire victims.

72. The residents of New Street examine the rubble. To the left of the lamp-post can be seen the sign of the *Blacksmith's Arms* – all of the building that remained intact!

A. Kenplenny

GENERAL VIEW OF THE RUINS

INSURANCE

William Cook's Farm—on which the fire began.

Hunting for household treasures.

73. The *Daily Graphic* newspaper produced their artist's impressions of the disastrous New Street fire later in the week.

74. The London and County Banking Company's premises, Bridge Street, *c*.1870. The man on the right of the doorway wearing the top hat was Mr. A. Foster, the manager. To the extreme right is the shop of Mr. C. Tredgold, bootmaker, at 3 High Street.

75. The *White Hart* Hotel, Bridge Street, *c*.1898. The hotel dates back to 1671. In the 18th and early 19th centuries it was an important coaching inn. Note the letters C.T.C. and badge – the Cyclists' Touring Club's insignia – on the face of the building. To the left of the hotel, hidden by the trees, was Dugey's furniture store.

76. Another view of the *White Hart* Hotel, *c*.1912, with hire cars parked outside. The C.T.C. badge has been obliterated as the hotel no longer sought the cyclists' trade. Just to the right of the hotel is Clark Bros., fishmongers and fruiterers, who later moved to premises on the other side of the street.

77. The Andover Co-operative Society Limited opened this store at 35 and 37 Bridge Street in 1901. In 1909 the Society moved across the street to a larger store, which was altered and extended in 1923. The Co-op ceased trading at these premises in 1986.

78. The Andover Co-operative Society's store in 1924. In the background on the left is the Andover Town railway station signalbox and the level crossing gates.

79. W. G. Latimer outside his boot repairer's shop at 19 Bridge Street in 1907. The business later moved to 18 Junction Road and H. J. Gifford, an electrical and radio engineer, took over at the Bridge Street premises. P. Squire (Andover) Ltd., electrical, radio and television engineers, occupy the shop today.

80. A general view of Bridge Street, *c.*1906. The large building on the right housed the town's free library and small museum until the early 1970s. In front of the library are the offices of C. K. Reynolds and Co., auctioneers and valuers.

81. Carters watering their horses in the River Anton, Bridge Street, *c.*1901. The town mill in the background, one of six Andover mills named in Domesday Book, was rebuilt in 1764 by John Gibbs, wheelwright. It closed in the late 1960s and has been converted into a restaurant and bar.

82. Webb and Wilson's butcher's shop, 11 Bridge Street, *c*.1919. The special display was for the annual 'Meat Show Night' held just before Christmas for many years. All the town's butchers and poulterers took part in the event and the town band, followed by a large crowd, would visit, and play at each shop in turn.

Bridge Street, and Post Office, Andover.

83.   Bridge Street, *c*.1917. The building with the tower on the left is the General Post Office, opened in 1913. The garage on the right was run by H. P. Moore and Sons, and was taken over in the early 1920s by Wessex Motors Ltd. In later years it was Henley's, before the area was redeveloped a decade ago. Safeway's food store now occupies the site. Just beyond the garage was the *New Railway* Inn.

84. Members of one of the town's oldest friendly societies pose to have their picture taken at the rear of the *New Railway* Inn, Bridge Street, *c.*1920. The Tunbridge Wells Equitable Friendly Society – it has dropped the 'Southern Eastern Counties' from its title – still exists today. Seated first on the left is William Viney, a well-known retired Andover businessman, who was still a paid-up member in 1991!

85. The Wesleyan Methodist church, Bridge Street, *c*.1919. The church was opened and dedicated on Thursday, 19 April 1906.

86. The Andover Lighting and Power Company's showroom in Bridge Street, *c*.1908. The town's gasworks were built by the company in 1838 and on 15 October that same year the mayor, Thomas Heath, lit the first gas lamp in the High Street. To celebrate the event the shareholders dined at the *George* Hotel afterwards.

87. Workmen erecting the town's first gas-holder in 1902. When completed it had a 250,000 cubic feet capacity.

88. An aerial view of the town's gasworks, c.1924. The works can be seen at the top of the picture. The rows of houses form part of South Street. In the centre of the picture is the *Wellington* Inn where Winchester Street (right) runs into Winchester Road, at the turning to Old Winton Road.

89. The gasworks, which were situated by the town station railway yard off Bridge Street, c.1911. The buildings and gas-holders have long since been demolished and gas is supplied through underground pipes from Southampton.

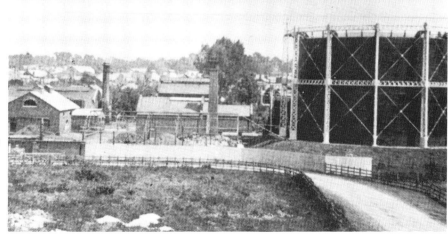

90. The Andover Corps of the Salvation Army had visits from two senior officials in 1904. In August Commissioner Railton, of Headquarters staff, was given a civic welcome. Later in the year the Army's leader, General Booth, came to Andover. Here he is being driven along Bridge Street on 31 October 1904. The General had been met on his arrival in the town by the mayor (Councillor W. C. McLoughlin) and members of the council. During his stay he attended a service of dedication and blessing at the Adelaide Assembly Rooms, which was attended by several hundred people.

91. The Chief Scout, General Sir H. Baden Powell (later Lord Baden Powell) and Lady Powell visited the town on Thursday, 28 April 1916. He is seen here reviewing the district scouts and wolf cubs in the High Street, watched by hundreds of onlookers. The parade was under the direction of District Scoutmaster F. Elton and the Chief Scout was welcomed by the District Commissioner, Mr. W. P. Clarke.

92. Andover Town station, Bridge Street, *c.*1904. The line between the town and Southampton was axed by Lord Beeching in 1964, and the station buildings were demolished soon afterwards. Where the porters are standing on the track is now part of the town's inner link road system, built in the late 1960s.

93. A steam rail car pulls into Andover Town station, *c.*1906. The single-carriage rail car operated from Andover Junction via Andover Town and the Clatfords to Fullerton Junction, and via Wherwell, Longparish and through Harewood Forest to Hurstbourne Priors station, before returning to Andover Junction. It carried mainly local workers and schoolchildren.

94.   The railway line from London to Andover was opened in 1854, and extended to Salisbury in 1857. This view of Andover Junction station in 1906 was taken at the time when the station was an important rail link. Besides the West Country route, trains from Cheltenham to Southampton, via Swindon, used the station, and there was a branch line to the Army garrison at Tidworth.

95.   The staff of Andover Junction station, *c.*1903-4.

96.   A view of the station and its marshalling yards, looking towards London, *c.*1904. The signal box in the foreground and other buildings, as well as some of the tracks, have been removed following the closure of the Cheltenham-Southampton route in 1964 and the modernisation of the West Country route.

97.   In the 137 years of its existence only a handful of crashes have occurred at Andover Junction Station. The worst of these was on 13 October 1914 when a 50-truck goods train from Exeter smashed into a line of 40 stationary trucks. Most of the trucks were derailed and the contents scattered over the tracks. The Exeter train was carrying livestock, and farm and garden produce. Several bullocks and cows were killed, and those that escaped wandered off between the wrecked trucks before being rounded up.

98.   The engine of the wrecked Exeter goods train in the 1914 crash.

99. A similar accident occurred at the station on 6 October 1916, again involving a fast goods train from Exeter. No-one was injured but several trucks were derailed and smashed.

100. The level crossing gates at the Town station in Bridge Street during the 1920s. Motorists using the main A303 route through the town to the West Country in the 1950s and early 1960s well remember the serious traffic holdups during the summer holiday season when the gates were closed. A bypass to the south of the town was opened in 1969.

101. Western Road, leading off from the level crossing gates in Bridge Street, as seen during the great snowstorm on 25 April 1908. Grafton House, on the left, has been demolished and replaced by blocks of flats and a garage. In the background is the old Toll House.

102. The old Toll House which stood at the junction of the Weyhill and Salisbury roads with Western Road, *c.*1900. It was pulled down in the mid-1930s when improvements were carried out at the road junction.

103. Salisbury Road, *c.*1914, showing no signs of development on either side of the road. Note the recruiting poster on the wall of the old Toll House.

104. Millway Road, between the Weyhill and Salisbury roads, *c.*1906. It was one of the first roads to be developed west of the River Anton after the 1870s.

105.   Particulars of sale of Hillside, Weyhill Road, 1885. The house was built for the late Harry Footner, the first town clerk of Andover, in 1843. The name of the house was changed to Beech Hurst in the mid-1890s and a wing added to the building. In September 1947 Andover Borough Council purchased the property for use as the Council's main offices. With 10 acres of land the house cost £8,000. In late 1990 Beech Hurst was demolished to make way for the Test Valley Borough Council's new headquarters.

106.   A sketch of Hillside when it was offered for sale in 1885.

107.   Beech Hurst as it looked when put up for auction in 1909. The wing that was added can be seen on the left.

108.   Some of the guests who attended the official dinner given by the Mayor of Andover (Councillor B. B. Pond) in the Guildhall, to celebrate the Coronation of King George V on 22 June 1911.

109. London Street was the scene of this procession celebrating Queen Victoria's Jubilee on 28 June 1887. Hundreds of people took part including the mayor (Alderman F. C. Ellen), the borough council, friendly societies and other organisations. Afterwards nearly 5,000 men, women and children enjoyed an open-air dinner in the High Street.

110. Workmen putting the finishing touches to the ceremonial arches at the junction of London Street and Winchester Street in 1893. The arches were built by Messrs. Beale and Son as part of the celebrations for the wedding of the Duke and Duchess of York (later King George V and Queen Mary).

111.   The procession which preceded the start of the Andover and District Band of Hope Union Fête at the Walled
Meadow on 27 August 1913. The procession had formed in the Vigo Road Recreation Ground and was about to turn from
Newbury Street into the upper High Street when this shot was taken.

112.   London Street (formerly King's Head Street) at the junction with East Street, *c.*1901. The old building protruding on the right, selling 'Nutley's Winchester Ales', a local brew, is the site of the present *King's Head* public house. On the immediate right was the workshop of H. G. Cable, a carpenter and wheelwright, which was pulled down when the new *King's Head* was built.

113. Dene Road, leading off London Street by the side of the *King's Head, c.*1904. Nearly all the old cottages have disappeared over the years to be replaced by new buildings.

114. The staff of Edward Chamberlain's gun shop on the corner of Bridge Street and Winchester Street, *c.*1919. The shop was opened in the late 1860s by Charles Edward Clarke. In a trade directory for 1895 appears 'Edward Chamberlain, gun and fishing tackle maker, breech-loading revolvers; sole agent for Newcastle patent chilled shot, 1 Bridge Street.' It closed in the mid-1960s.

115. Winchester Street, *c.*1898. The building on the left is the Wesleyan Chapel built in 1824. Since 1906 it has been used by the Andover Corps of the Salvation Army as its Citadel. Opposite the Citadel is the *Lamb* Inn, one of the town's older public houses.

116. The start of South Street from lower Winchester Street, *c.*1906. All the houses on either side of the street have been replaced in the intervening years, on the right of the street by Andover Police Station, opened in 1959, and recently-built office blocks. The other side is now a car park.

117. The Ladies' Walk, *c*.1904, laid out in 1785 by the Enclosure Award Commissioners in conjunction with the Corporation of Andover. Over 120 trees were planted along its route in 1863 to commemorate the wedding of the Prince of Wales and Princess Alexandra. A road – the old Micheldever Road (A303) – was cut through the walk in 1840.

118. The iron bridge linking the two sections of the Ladies' Walk, *c*.1916. The bridge was built by Messrs. Taskers, of Anna Valley.

119. A view of the town taken from the Shepherd's Spring area in 1904. No longer open water meadows, the area in the background is taken up by the Cricklade College complex, the town's sports centre and various office blocks, all built between the late 1960s and the 1980s.

120.   William Walters standing outside his butcher's shop in Chantry Street, *c.*1901. Next to the shop is the *Phoenix* Inn, demolished in the 1960s. Mr. Walters ceased trading in about 1904 and the premises later became a wholesale stationery and confectionery shop run by Mr. F. R. Simpson. It has been restored and is now a bric-a-brac and curio shop. All the buildings on the right have been demolished.

121. Chantry Street, *c*.1898, looking up towards St Mary's parish church. The two little boys on the left are standing outside J. W. Carr's confectionery shop. The properties on the left have been replaced by the town's sports centre, an office block and a car park.

122. Marlborough Street, *c*.1920, leading to the upper High Street and the turning to Chantry Street. This peaceful setting, just under half a mile from the town centre, presents a different scene today. On the right is a large car park serving the sports centre and the Cricklade College complex. To the left is the T.S.B.'s new spacious headquarters.

123. Vigo Road, formerly London Road, *c.*1910. The houses in the background were known as 'Silkweavers Cottages'; the town's silk workers used to live there. The whole area was redeveloped in 1982-3 with new homes and a block of old people's flats.

124. Newbury Street, *c*.1912, one of the oldest and shortest streets in the town. In the foreground on the right is Priory House and next to it is the vicarage. At the junction beyond, roads lead to East Street (right), Vigo Road (ahead) and New Street (left). A firm of solicitors occupies the old vicarage today and Priory House has been converted into offices.

125. Andover's first theatre opened in Newbury Street at Easter 1803. The theatre was run by a Mr. Thornton but audiences were not large enough to meet the running costs and it eventually closed in the mid-1830s. This print was published by Thomas Woodfall in 1804.

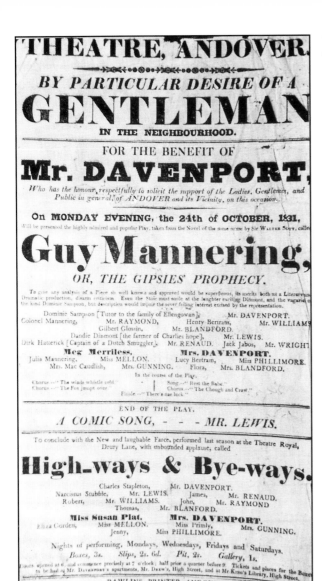

126. A poster advertising the actors appearing at the Andover Theatre in 1831.

127. The Electric Picture Hall – Andover's first cinema –
opened in West Street in 1911. It changed to the New Theatre
in 1926 and many live shows were presented on stage in the
1920s and 1930s. Later renamed The Rex, it was closed in
1956. For a few years it was a furniture store, before being
demolished in the 1960s to make way for the new shopping
centre.

128. Another picture of the cinema taken in the early 1920s, with the doormen and page boys.

129. The Palace Cinema, Junction Road, opened on 20 December 1926. The building was designed by Mr. F. Henshaw, a well-known Andover architect, and built by Sturgess Bros. of Ludgershall. In the early 1930s it was renamed the Odeon after being purchased by the Rank Organisation. It is now the Mecca leisure, social and bingo hall.

130. The old Post Office in the High Street, *c*.1900. It was closed in 1913 when the new General Post Office was opened in Bridge Street. Montagu Burton Ltd., the tailors, have occupied the site since the early 1930s; the present shop is named 'Principles'.

131. Some of the postmen and messenger boys who were at the old High Street premises, *c*.1908.

132. Rooksbury Mill, pictured here *c.*1904, off Salisbury Road, was one of the six Andover mills mentioned in Domesday Book. For many years now the mill has been a private residence.

133. Anton Mill, *c.*1906, off Barlow's Lane – another of the mills named in Domesday Book. Formerly Barlow's Mill and Pitt's Mill, it was purchased by Hovis Ltd. in 1899 and assumed the name of Anton Mill. The mill and the millhouse were demolished in 1974.

134. *(Above)* A general view of the Waterloo Iron Works, *c*.1903. Built in 1815, Messrs. Taskers' premises at Anna valley, on the outskirts of the town, gave employment to hundreds of Andover's skilled tradesmen, labourers and office staff over the years, before it was closed in 1984. The works buildings have been replaced by a private housing estate.

135. *(Left)* An advertisement appearing in a trade directory for 1870, detailing the various implements and machinery made at Taskers.

136. *(Right)* These skilled boilermakers at Taskers paused for a few moments to have their picture taken, *c*.1888.

137. Workmen from the old carpenters' shop at Taskers, *c*.1888.

138. Men at work in Taskers' foundry, *c*.1888.

139. During World War One, Taskers switched some of its production to munitions work. These women workers are engaged in filling artillery shells, *c*.1915.

140.   The Anton Laundry, Marlborough Street, *c*.1909. The laundry, established in 1895, is the only one of three major laundries in the town still in business today. The Andover Family Laundry, George Yard, ceased trading in the early 1960s, and the Southern Fyne Laundry Ltd., London Street, closed in the mid-1970s.

141.   Described in an old Andover Almanac as 'one of the principal industries in the town giving employment to some 70 hands', this picture of the Anton Laundry was taken around the turn of the century.

142. Andover Cottage Hospital, *c.*1904, situated in Junction Road. Built in 1876-7 at a cost of £2,500, a further £1,600 was spent extending the hospital in 1906. Patients were treated there until the Andover War Memorial Hospital was opened in 1926. It then became a children's clinic and dental centre. The old buildings were demolished in the late 1980s.

143. Andover War Memorial Hospital, Charlton Road, opened by Field Marshal the Viscount Allenby in June 1926. The £16,000 needed to build the hospital was raised entirely by public subscription. The man behind the scheme was Mr. Edmund Parsons, a well-known Andover businessman and historian. He was secretary of the hospital fund-raising committee, and his unstinting efforts were rewarded when he was made a Freeman of the Borough.

144. The Andover Union, *c.*1906, situated opposite the Cottage Hospital in Junction Road. Built in 1836 the old workhouse gained notoriety in 1846 when an enquiry was held into the treatment and working conditions of the inmates. Known as the 'Andover Workhouse Scandal', it attracted national publicity at the time. It became St John's Hospital for the elderly in 1948. Today it forms an annexe to the Cricklade College and is used for further education courses.

145. This drawing of the Andover Union was published shortly after the building was completed at a cost of £6,100. It could accommodate up to 300 persons but only 111 men, women and children moved in on the day it opened – Saturday, 25 March 1836.

ANDOVER "UNION" WAS PLACE OF HORROR

No 438.   WEEK ENDING SATURDAY, SEPTEMBER 6, 1845.

THE ANDOVER BASTILE.

THE POOR PICKING THE BONES TO LIVE
See our Leader.

THE COMMISSION OF INQUIRY DISCUSSING THE SUBJECT OVER A GOOD DINNER.

(From the Newspapers)

Workhouse Atrocities.—Just before the Prorogation of Parliament, Mr. Wakley asked Sir James Graham if he had heard "that the paupers of a Union in Hampshire were employed in crushing bones, and that while so employed they were engaged in quarrelling with each other for the bones, in extracting marrow from them, and in gnawing off meat from the extremities. . . ."

146. Published in 1845 in *The Penny Satirist*, a London newspaper, this cartoon offers a grim commentary upon the shocking conditions at the Andover Union at the time of the inquiry. The Commission of Inquiry's findings, issued in 1846, told how the inmates were ill-treated and starved. Men and boys would pick the rotting meat bones that they were forced to grind for hours every day to make a form of fertiliser, sold to local farmers. Some even tried to eat the marrow inside the bones in an attempt to satisfy their hunger.

147. Members of the Andover Volunteer Fire Brigade with their horse-drawn manual pump, *c.*1885. The horses used to pull the pump were kept in a field adjacent to the engine shed.

148. Outside the Andover Fire Station in East Street the brigade's 'Steamer' pump drawn by four horses, *c.*1904. On the right is the hose cart with its two horses. Captain Arthur Beale, who was in charge of the brigade from 1902-35, is standing on the left in his full fire officer's uniform.

149. A crowd soon gathered when this Army biplane, complete with Maxim gun, force-landed at Andover Down on 10 September 1912. It was probably the first armed military aircraft to come down in the Andover area. The photographer on the spot was Fred Wright.

150. It was Fred Wright who was quickly at the scene when this aircraft crashed to the south-west of the town in the following year. The pilot, an Army major, escaped with cuts and bruises and walked to a nearby house for help.

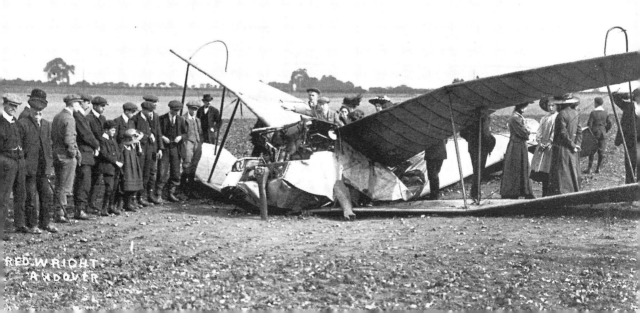

151. Wykeham House High School for Girls, Western Road, c.1909. It remained a school, under different proprietors, until 1936, when it became the Andover Conservative Club. The club bought the property for £1,850 and £5 legal costs, and still owns the building today.

East Street Establishment,

ANDOVER.

MISS M. E. MOORE,

Principal,

Assisted by experienced Governesses and eminent Masters.

The advantages offered in this Establishment are numerous: kind treatment and careful training, in addition to a sound Education, home comforts, liberal table, diet good and unlimited.

The House has been occupied as a Ladies' Seminary during the last 43 years; it is healthily situated, and has undergone considerable improvement since in the possession of the present Proprietress.

REFERENCES TO PARENTS OF PUPILS.

TERMS ON APPLICATION.

152. An advertisement appearing in a local directory for 1870 for Miss M. E. Moore's school in East Street.

153. The old Andover Grammar School for Boys, New Street, *c.*1902. The building now houses the town's museum, run by Hampshire County Council. Founded in 1569, the school was rebuilt in 1773, with additions being made in 1848. New classrooms were added in 1888 but since that time the outward appearance of the building has remained much the same. The school moved to new buildings in Weyhill Road in 1925 and girls were admitted for the first time. It is now the John Hanson comprehensive.

154. One of the classrooms at the old Andover Grammar School, added in 1888.

The Memorial of

JOHN HANSON

Gent: Founder of the
Free-school. A.D: 1569.

No Marble Statue is to thee erected,
No tonnie of Alabaster Touch, or Brafs;
These things by thee while living were neg
And thy Survivors all have let them pafs.

O but yet live! why should thy name decay
Till Heav'n & Earth & all things pass away.

And live thou shalt. Thy schools Gratuity
Arts lasting maintenance, two hundred poun
Shall give thy Name its perp-tuity;
Students in Arts shall thence lay praises foun

Heav'ns hand upon thy Sun put out thy light
Yet fo as now to make thy Fame more bright

156. The National School, in East Street (now Andover Primary School), c.1900. The school was started in 1818 but the present buildings were designed in 1859. Plans to rebuild the school in recent years have failed to materialise although additions and improvements have been carried out to the present buildings.

157. The British School, New Street, c.1902, was started in Rack Close in 1834. It moved to New Street in the late 1840s and adopted that street's name as its title around 1932. In 1954 the name was changed to Norman Gate Primary School. It was closed in 1966 with the opening of the new Balkesbury School, off Salisbury Road, and the buildings were demolished to make way for road improvements.

158. Some of the boys who attended the British School, c.1914. Standing on the left is the head teacher, Mr. A. E. Daniels, who became the Mayor of Andover in 1935.

159.   Russian bears performing their tricks in the High Street, c.1906. Circus artists from the Ukraine brought the bears over to tour England. They stayed at small public houses, sleeping with their animals in an outhouse or barn. The young girl behind the larger bear took a collection from the crowd at the end of the performance.

160.   Guides taking part in a first aid contest at a District Guide Rally, held at the Walled Meadow in 1918 or 1919. A travelling fair can be seen in the background with swinging boats and roundabouts.

161.   Workmen employed by Marden, Ball and Co., builders of Fareham, rebuilding the old Capital and Counties Bank at 22 High Street, 1919. On completion of the work Lloyds Bank moved into the premises and still remain there today.

ANDOVER F.C. 1890.

Back Row Standing: Mr. Fred Browne, E. Fleming, C. Simkins, W. R. Ponting,
F. Wheeler, Mr. H. J. Humber. Sitting: F. Colebrook, A. Smith, W. Turle, F. Quinton,
H. Webb. On Ground: J. Hendley, H. Milborne.

162. Andover Football Club in 1890. The club, now over 100 years old, played on the Walled Meadow until 1989 when it moved to a new ground on the outskirts of the town.

163. Andover F.C.'s club mascot in the 1911-12 era was 'Billy the Ram'. It belonged to Mr. C. Simkins of Old Winton Road, a keen Andover supporter. The ram used to follow Mr. Simkins around just like a dog. Billy would always lead the team onto the field before a match.

"Billy" the Ram which acts as Mascot to the Andover Football Club.

"Daily Mirror" Photograph.

164.   Members of a women's Christian
organisation in the High Street (*c*.1917)
raising money to provide comforts for the
troops and funds for canteens. The wounded
soldier with the sling is playing a barrel
organ.

165.   Two Andover ladies, Miss Nuttall and
Mrs. Cook, selling charity flags in the High
Street to two Australian soldiers, *c*.1917. The
shops in the background were the
International Stores, now Peacock's, and
Mair's, newsagents, run today by the
Charlton News.

166. Crowds gathered in the High Street in March 1913 for one of the fund-raising events to buy more aircraft for the war effort. So successful was the savings week that £57,000 was subscribed by the townspeople, enough to buy 20 aircraft. Note the aircraft flying over the Guildhall.

167. An aerial view of the Royal Air Force Station, Andover, taken on 13 October 1918. Fighter and bomber aircraft can be seen parked on the airfield. Opened in 1916, the R.A.F. station was closed in June 1977. Most of the buildings shown in the aerial picture are gone but today the Army has its Logistics Executive Headquarters on the site.

168. Members of the Red Cross and other voluntary organisations, along with ex-servicemen, attending a dinner at the Drill Hall, East Street, during the peace celebrations in 1919. The Drill Hall, built in 1908, was destroyed by fire in the mid-1980s when it was known as the Country Bumpkin Club.

169. One of the dozens of pictures taken by Fred Wright of the peace celebrations parade in the High Street in 1919.

170. Watched by a large crowd, soldiers and volunteers take part in a tent-erecting contest, at the peace celebration fête held in the Walled Meadow in 1919.

171. One of the decorated carts taking part in a parade at the peace celebration fête, 1919.

172. On 22 May 1922, King George V and Queen Mary arrived at Andover Junction station before making the short journey by car to Enham Village Centre on the outskirts of the town. The centre was opened in 1919 for the treatment and rehabilitation of severely handicapped ex-servicemen of World War One. The king and queen toured the village, stopping to talk to many of its residents. With them was the Duke of York (extreme left) who later became King George VI.

173. In June 1926 the Prince of Wales, later King Edward VIII, paid a brief visit to Andover. He was welcomed by the mayor, Alderman B. C. Kendall, outside the Guildhall and introduced to some of the senior members of the council. The Prince left to tour Enham Village Centre but before catching his train back to London he visited the Andover War Memorial Hospital, in Charlton Road. The hospital had been officially opened earlier in the day, and the Prince of Wales signed the visitors' book.

174. The unveiling of the War Memorial on 5 May 1920. A petition to have it moved from the front of the Guildhall – where it was felt it was being desecrated – was successful, and in 1956 it was re-erected in the Garden of Remembrance at St Mary's.

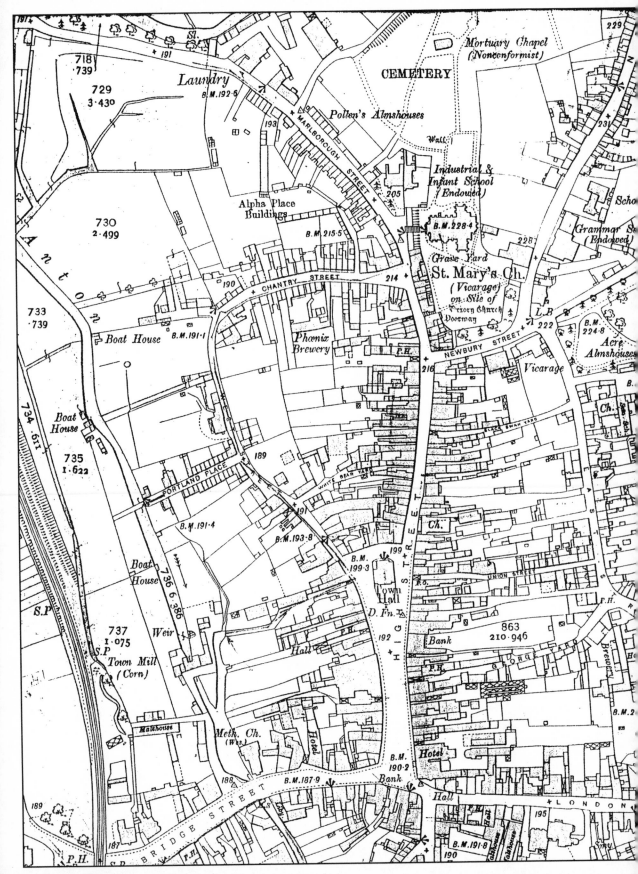

Map of Andover, 1910